Living at a Lighthouse

Oral history is remembering . . .

Looking across the Kalamazoo River channel at his old homeplace, the Kalamazoo River lighthouse in Saugatuck, Michigan, in about 1943, Joe Sheridan stood with his son Richard and nephew Jack and told them of his boyhood at the lighthouse. Joe Sheridan is deceased and the Kalamazoo River lighthouse no longer exists, but members of the Sheridan family still share the memories of life at a lighthouse. (Photo by James E. Sheridan. Courtesy of the Sheridan family).

Living at a Lighthouse

Oral Histories from the Great Lakes

GREAT LAKES LIGHTHOUSE KEEPERS ASSOCIATION

Edited by LuAnne Gaykowski Kozma

Printed in the United States of America.
First Edition.

ISBN 0-940767-00-7
Library of Congress Catalog Card Number 87-80329

Grateful acknowledgment is made to Harper's Magazine for permission to reprint the previously published material: Photograph "Home of a Lighthouse-Keeper" by Frances B. Johnston and excerpts from "Through Inland Seas" by Louise Morgan Sill. Copyright © 1904 by Harper's Magazine. All rights reserved. Reprinted from the April issue by special permission.

This publication is made possible in part by a grant from Michigan Council for the Humanities and their sponsor, the National Endowment for the Humanities.

Design by Tom and LuAnne Kozma.

Printed on 60# Warren paper by Harlo Printing, 50 Victor, Detroit, Michigan.

ON THE COVER: A postcard depicting Little Point Sable lighthouse in Oceana County, Michigan, and unknown lighthouse family, circa 1900. (Courtesy of Gary Kurylo).

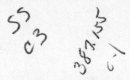

Contents

Acknowledgments

We wish to thank the people interviewed and their families for generously sharing their reminiscences, time, and photographs with us and for making a lasting contribution to Great Lakes lighthouse history that only they can give.

We also thank our financial sponsors: the Michigan Council for the Humanities and their sponsor, the National Endowment for the Humanities; the Detroit Area Yachtswomen, whose contribution early on in our research allowed us to create an interviewing handbook especially for the project; and Great Lakes Lighthouse Keepers Association (GLLKA) members through whose personal donations, membership dues, and fundraising efforts much of this project has been funded.

We appreciate the advice and efforts of our consultants: Charles K. Hyde, of Wayne State University, Department of History; Janet Langlois, of Wayne State University Folklore Archive and Department of English; and Glenn Ruggles, of Michigan Oral History Council.

"Living at a Lighthouse: Oral Histories from the Great Lakes" has been a group effort of GLLKA members from all over the Great Lakes. The participants have volunteered over 800 hours of their time and contributed nearly $4,000 in in-kind donations of travel costs, materials, film, phone calls, postage, and services. Without their help and sincere interest in lighthouse history, this project would not have been possible. We gratefully acknowledge interviewers Jean D. Gertz (Appleton, WI), Nancy Johnson (Birmingham, MI), Karen McDonnell-Dziesinski (Whitehall, MI), Dick Moehl (Pinckney, MI), Eva J. Price (South Bend, IN), Ted C. Richardson (St. Clair, MI), Steve Sheridan (Saugatuck, MI), Jinx Sisson (Grand Rapids, MI), Darla Van Hoey (Southfield, MI), and

Mike Vogel (Buffalo, NY), and indexers and transcribers Brenda Marr (Lansing, MI) and Lois Mason (Mt. Clemens, MI).

Also appreciated are John Tregembo (Plymouth, MI) and Leon DeRosia (Bay City, MI) for demonstrating a sample interview to the public at our 1985 Lake Huron conference at Port Austin, MI. Similarly, Joseph St. Andre (Lake Linden, MI), Don Nelson (Marquette, MI), and James Goudreau (Gulliver, MI) shared their lighthouse experiences at our 1986 Lake Superior conference in Munising, MI. We also wish to thank the people who were interviewed for the project and do not appear in this book, including Edith Bates (New Buffalo, MI), Robert Clark (Rockford, MI), Joanne Climie (Crestwood, IL), Earline E. Hammer (Hamburg, NY), Ralph Hill (Kenmore, NY), and Betty Williams (Birmingham, MI).

GLLKA treasurers Mike Van Hoey and Nancy Johnson were invaluable for their assistance with the bookkeeping and finances. The GLLKA board of directors and conference coordinators gave continuous and enthusiastic support of the project. And lastly, thanks to Tom Kozma, who assisted me in the field and at the computer.

LuAnne Gaykowski Kozma
Oral History Project Director
February 1987

Introduction

People who lived at Great Lakes lighthouses have stories to tell. There are stories of daily life and work, of family members and family traditions, and of events both common and unusual. Lighthouse keeping was more than a career; it was a way of life for an entire family. A complete account of lighthouse history cannot be found in the written records left behind, in the keepers' log books and the government reports. The memories, family stories, and first-hand accounts of daily life and events as told by people who lived that experience add greatly to our knowledge of the social history of life at the lighthouses.

To help document and preserve that part of history, the Great Lakes Lighthouse Keepers Association (GLLKA) began an oral history project in April 1985 entitled "Living at a Lighthouse: Oral Histories from the Great Lakes," with grants from the Michigan Council for the Humanities and the Detroit Area Yachtswomen. People who once lived or worked at Great Lakes lighthouses were interviewed on tape by a GLLKA volunteer. The tapes were indexed and then donated to the Wayne State University Folklore Archive in Detroit, Michigan. A copy was given to the Lake Michigan Maritime Museum in South Haven, Michigan. People interviewed for the project also shared their reminiscences at GLLKA conferences.

This publication is another way in which the people interviewed share their stories. It is not meant to be a comprehensive history of all Great Lakes lighthouses, (and only U.S. lighthouses are considered here), or the history of lighthouse structures, nor is it the history of any one family.

The excerpts in this book are from interviews conducted from April 1985 to March 1986. Interviews usually took place in the

individual's home and occasionally at a lighthouse. The
volunteers spent many hours preparing to interview by learning
oral history techniques, becoming familiar with lighthouse
history, and getting acquainted with the person through
correspondence and phone calls. Some individuals were
interviewed by a member of their own family. Those
interviewed spent time preparing for the interview, too, by
gathering together their family memorabilia, and filling out
"personal data forms" to accompany the tape-recorded
interviews. Interview questions fell in these categories: family
history; work of a keeper; work of family members; lighthouse
careers; social customs and recreation; educating and raising
children; foodways; sense of place; and family traditions and
customs.

The stories that emerged from these interviews reveal many
themes. The interviewees describe how the family conformed
to government rules, their dedication to duty, and the value of
resourcefulness and cooperation at an isolated place. They also
talk of the many escapades they had as children. Perhaps what
marked their lifestyle from their neighbors' the most was the
need to keep the lighthouse dwellings clean to pass inspections
by government officials. "Inspection stories"--anecdotes about
visits by the inspectors and how the family prepared for an
inspection--are well-remembered and told often. And like all
families, they tell of tragedies, mishaps, humorous incidents,
courageous characters, and family customs.

Prior to 1939, lighthouses were under the jurisdiction of the
U.S. Lighthouse Service. In that year, the Lighthouse Service
was incorporated into the U. S. Coast Guard. Some keepers
then chose to join the Coast Guard, while others chose to
continue working but remained civilians. The people
interviewed for this project lived at lighthouses during each of
these administrative periods.

How the Interviews are Edited

The excerpts do not represent entire interviews. Only portions have been included for the purposes of this publication. Some editing was done for clarity, while maintaining the original, conversational quality of the spoken word. For example, some false starts and "crutch" words (like "uh") have been removed unless they provide useful information or meaning. Some excerpts on the same topic appear together as if they occured in sequence, but deletions are always noted either by an ellipsis (. . .) or by switching to another topic.

To retain the original sound of the speakers' words, grammar was not corrected. Alternate pronunciations and contractions are used (if the person said "can't" it was not changed to "cannot"), but no attempt was made to reproduce dialect by using unconventional spellings (for example, even if a person's dialect made the word "wash" sound like "warsh" it would appear as "wash").

A broken sentence is indicated by a dash (--). Editorial or clarifying comments by the editor, transcriber, or interviewer appear in brackets [ ]. Only parenthetical statements by an interviewee during the interview are in parentheses ( ). Except where noted otherwise, all interview excerpts were transcribed by the editor. Interviewees and interviewers reviewed the excerpts and made factual and spelling changes where necessary.

For easier reading, the editor's remarks are in this typeface. They serve to connect the interview excerpts and are kept to a minimum so that the speakers' own words are emphasized. Readers are reminded that the excerpts are the interviewees' spoken--not written--words.

The Tape Collection

GLLKA considers the cassette tapes of these interviews the primary sources. The tapes themselves are not edited or "corrected." This publication and any transcripts of the tapes are simply written interpretations of the original interviews. Researchers are encouraged to use the tapes to make their own transcripts. Other materials accompany each tape-recorded interview, such as family history information, newspaper clippings, and indexes to the tapes. An updated list of the oral history tape collection is available by writing GLLKA.

To use the research collection contact:

> Wayne State University Folklore Archive
> 448 Purdy Library, Wayne State University
> Detroit, MI 48202   (313) 577-4053

or: Lake Michigan Maritime Museum
> P.O. Box 534
> South Haven, MI 49090   (616) 637-8078

Range lights, beacons, fog-bells, storm-signals,--there is no end to them, nor to the brave, steady souls who keep them alight and never falter in the long and lonely performance of this duty. For the lakes are rich in capes, islands, and dangerous channels, beautiful as a dream by day--a dream of blue water and lustrous green isles wooded to their edges--but treacherous by night; and the light-keepers of the Great Lakes deserve a volume to themselves.

> *--Louise Morgan Sill*
> *"Through Inland Seas"*
> *Harper's Monthly*
> *April 1904*

Bud Richards being interviewed in his home in Port Hope, Michigan, on June 11, 1985. (Photo by Darla Van Hoey).

Leland L. "Bud" Richards

Bud Richards was born in 1901 at the Pointe Aux Barques lighthouse in Port Austin, Michigan, on Lake Huron. His father, Peter L. Richards, was assistant keeper there from 1899 to 1905 and served as keeper until 1939. Bud lived with his family at Pointe Aux Barques until he went to college in the 1920s. After a career as an educator and school administrator, he now lives in Port Hope, Michigan. He was interviewed on June 11, 1985.

(Interviewer: Darla Van Hoey; assisting with interview: Ted C. Richardson).

In describing his father's work, Bud points out the importance of checking the light's characteristic signal and taking care of the lens.

They had a stop watch. And they always timed the lens. . . . because the light was supposed to be on three seconds and off seven. When a boat sees that, they know what light it is.

. . . Oh, he cleaned the lens everyday. He had a cloth there that he kept the lens clean, dusted it. He didn't let anyone up there, either, where the lens were. They'll always want to touch it. And when you touch brass, you leave marks. And then you got a job taking it off. . . . No, I never [cleaned] it. He always did it.

Bud's father took his duties very seriously and was proud of Pointe Aux Barques' appearance. He kept the station looking good for the inspectors' benefit as well as for Sunday visitors.

. . . Oh, he was strong on maintenance. He really kept it up nice, didn't he? [to Mr. Richardson] A-Number One. It was a showplace. And on Sundays he spent most of the day in the tower showing people the light. He had to carry some down, too [laughs].

. . . Oh, he was strong on maintenance. He really kept it up nice. . . . A-Number One. It was a showplace. And on Sundays he spent most of the day in the tower showing people the light.

. . . Well they came and inspected every year. And that meant, too, that they inspected the assistant's house, too. My mother had to keep our house in A-Number One condition, inside, the beds, everything. You know, everything cleaned and all.

. . . They always had to be ready. But, I know a few times during my [time] up there, the inspector would come, the boats would come in, and my dad wouldn't be there. He'd be down town. . . . The assistant would take [the inspector] around

instead of my dad. As long as both of them weren't gone.
But, boy, on Sunday, I'll tell you, he was in that lighthouse
most of the time. It was beautiful. . . . [People came from] a
long ways away, like Flint, Port Huron, Detroit. Long ways
away! Oh, you might get an occasional one close, but usually
they were people you didn't know. . . . If I had been my dad,
I'd of gone up there with the first bunch and I'd of stayed right
there. Because he had to keep going up and down all the time.

Bud remembers that at some point, his father received
a salary of $125 each month as a lighthouse keeper.
And there were some fringe benefits.

Well, that was a lot of money then, with all the supplies you
got. You had to buy your own food and your clothes, but you
got all your supplies like soap and coal and kerosene. All that
sort of thing. And that ran in to quite a lot of money.

Once a year, the lighthouse boat--it was the ASPEN, the
AMARANTH, or the MARIGOLD--stopped out there about
two miles. They didn't dare come any closer. And they loaded
everything into their small boats, with the crew loading it. The
kerosene, and all the supplies. And that kerosene alone was a
big deal. It filled the oil house and it's--the oil house is ten or
twelve feet in diameter and higher than this room [about eight
feet], so, you know. It had shelves all the way around, see. It
was round. And they'd put the kerosene in there. And then,
of course, when we had to take the kerosene out of there in
five-gallon cans and carry it all the way to the top of the
lighthouse, that was something. That was really hard work.

Bud and his brothers were not expected to help their

father with the light, but when they were in their teens they were able to do so.

He never insisted that we do that at all. But, I always was willing, and so was my younger brother, to help him when he was sick or didn't feel good. . . . We did all the mowing. Hand mowers. And once in a while if it rained a few days and it got too high you'd have to tie a line on the mower and one pull it and the other push it in order to get it through. It was so hard to do.

Besides the maintenance of the grounds, a lighthouse family had many household chores.

Well, he had chickens and he had a couple of cows and a horse and we would feed those animals. Like the chickens, pick up eggs. And like me, for instance, occasionally I'd help my mother. She wasn't very big and strong. And I helped her a lot. . . . Like washing dishes and all that sort of thing. I didn't do any cooking.

Evening at the light station was a time for studying and playing parlor games.

Well, a lot of times we studied when we were going to school. And if we got stuck in arithmetic [my dad would] always help us. He was good at it. I don't know how he knew. I often wondered how he ever learned that stuff. He sure knew how to do those problems. Oh, we'd play a lot of dominoes, and stuff like that, you know, and cards. And there'd be three or four hands of us that could get at a table. Four of us: three boys and my dad. And we had a lot of fun.

Living at a Lighthouse

In later years that tradition continued. After Bud
married, he would bring his wife and daughters to visit
with his parents at the lighthouse.

We'd go up in the evening. We had a lot of nice evenings
there. He'd fix up a drink. We'd play dominoes. Usually
dominoes because my mother, she couldn't play cards. But we
played dominoes. We took the girls with us. And that's the
way it was. We had a lot of fun.

When Bud was a boy, the family's reading materials
included daily newspapers, books, and reference
books.

You got the *[Detroit] Free Press* every day, delivered by the
mailman up there. And, of course, [my dad] had certain
books. He always had a dictionary. He'd always look up
words or anything. He always had a dictionary there on his
desk.

At Pointe Aux Barques, the Richards family set aside
Sunday as a special day.

We went to church and Sunday school every Sunday. He
wouldn't let us play ball or we couldn't play checkers--that's
another game we played a lot, in particular--or any game on
Sunday at all. We observed the Sunday.

Being a lighthouse kid wasn't all work and no play, but
sometimes one had to be clever about it.

We had a little garden and we worked in it, too. We hoed it.
We did everything. We three [brothers]. One day, my dad
went to town and we made an agreement. He said, "Hoe the
garden." We said, "All right." There'd be three rows, you
know? Each one would get on a row and we'd go up to the
end which was next to the lake. Every time we'd get to the end
we'd strip off and jump in the lake. And we went in eighteen
times that afternoon! But we never told him until after we grew
up!

---

*Oh, the lake was off limits. He
really watched us, as far as the
lake was concerned, for fear that
there'd be a drowning.*

. . . Oh, the lake was off limits. He really watched us, as far
as the lake was concerned, for fear that there'd be a drowning.
And more than once my dad has, (when we were sleeping of
course), when the wind was offshore, would push the raft off
that we had made to push around in, and let it go. More than
once!

Apparently, Bud's father was equally clever. Bud
remembers another time when his father's ingenuity
served him well. During the Great Storm of 1913, he
kept the light burning in an unusual way.

The 1913 Storm was the worst storm that I had ever seen in my life. It wrecked every boat in the lake. And the ones that didn't sink or beach, why, it wrecked them. And during this storm we had then an oil wick. A lamp with an oil wick on it. And during this storm [my dad] would go up--he would anyway, every ten minutes, to look up to see if it was all right. And it started to dim, see. And he'd go up. And he made two or three trips up there before he found out what was wrong. And it was the vibration of the tower that was causing this wick to drop. So, he took a string and tied the wick and he didn't have any more trouble. Now that was really something.

Jim Sheridan, of Saugatuck, Michigan, in 1983. He wrote about his family's lighthouse keeping tradition in his book "Saugatuck Through the Years." (Photo ©1983 by James E. Sheridan. Used with permission).

James E. Sheridan
George F. Sheridan

Lighthouse keeping in the Sheridan family has spanned several generations. The following excerpts are from interviews with James E. Sheridan, of Saugatuck, Michigan, and his brother George F. Sheridan, of Mt. Clemens, Michigan. Jim was born in 1909 at the Michigan City, Indiana, lighthouse and George in 1911 at the Kalamazoo River light in Saugatuck, (both lights on Lake Michigan), where their father, George H. Sheridan, served in the U.S. Lighthouse Service. Their grandparents, Aaron A. and Julia Sheridan, were keepers at South Manitou Island lighthouse from 1866 to 1878. In addition, Aaron's cousins, Lyman F. and Phillip Sheridan, were Great Lakes keepers during the late nineteenth century.

(James E. Sheridan was interviewed on January 10, 1986 by his son, Steve Sheridan; George F. Sheridan was interviewed by Nancy P. Johnson on September 14, 1985).

George H. Sheridan began his career as a keeper in Chicago in about 1900. While there he married Sarah Unwin. In 1905 he was transferred to the light at Michigan City, Indiana, where they had their first two

George F. Sheridan stands next to framed photographs of his ancestors--many of whom were lighthouse keepers--in his Mt. Clemens, Michigan home, September 14, 1985. (Photo by Nancy P. Johnson).

sons, Joseph and James. Soon after Jim's birth, the
Sheridans moved to the Kalamazoo River light.

[Jim]: Well, I actually didn't live in Michigan City very long.
I was born in March. But the family moved because my father,
at Michigan City, was the assistant keeper. He was transferred
and moved to the lighthouse at Saugatuck, Michigan, at the
mouth of the Kalamazoo River. And during the period
between my birth and when I arrived in Saugatuck, shortly
after I was a mere babe in arms, my mother took me to Chicago
where her sister and family lived--(her mother was still living at
that time)--and she stayed there until, oh, almost the first of
June, late in May, visiting her mother. During that period from
March till June, my father was at the lighthouse in Saugatuck.
And the family who had lived there [at the lighthouse] were
moving to Saugatuck. The previous keeper was a man by the
name of Baker who was retiring. And he moved down to
Saugatuck, which at that time was two and a half miles away.

Because of the geography of the Saugatuck area,
traveling those few short miles from the lighthouse to
town was not easy.

[Jim]: In those days, the Kalamazoo River took a tremendous
circle around a large area to the north, then curled around to a
southerly point, and then out into the lake. This was known as
"the oxbow" or "the hairpin." . . . The federal government had
cut a new harbor through there so that, really, there were two
harbors there. It was cut through at a portion of the bend,
straight out into the lake, while the old entrance to the harbor
remained. And, actually, the lighthouse, then, that I lived in
was not of any value, as far as guiding people into the harbor
was concerned, because at that time there was a light at the end

of the new pier and no light at the old pier. . . . It continued to be used for five or six years after we got there.

. . . The lighthouse was not, really, all that far from town. It was about . . . two or three miles from town. But to get there was a difficult thing. There was no road between the lighthouse (which was not at the end of the pier, but it was close to the shore) and town. . . . To get from the lighthouse to town, you actually had to cross the Kalamazoo River twice. You had to cross the river at the lighthouse because the lighthouse was not on the same side as the path that went to town. Then you had to cross it again when you came to the upper end of the big bend or "oxbow." So, you always had to cross it twice, and we crossed it by boat in those days when we traveled from the lighthouse to town.

The Sheridans were somewhat isolated from neighbors and relatives in winter. But in summer, the Saugatuck area was busy with visitors and vacationing families.

[Jim]: In earlier days there was a considerable community near the lighthouse. It was a place called Singapore which, really, was quite a famous place. It was a lumber town. And it existed for about fifty years as an important lumber center. But before I ever got there, all the habitation in that area disappeared. There was only one family that lived close to the lighthouse and they were fishermen.

[George]: We stayed there winter and summer. . . . We had a lot of friends during the summer. As I said, the resorters were all around and the fishermen were there. But, I guess, probably in the winter months it's probably quite lonely.

The Kalamazoo River lighthouse and boathouse near Saugatuck, Michigan, circa 1910, when the Sheridans lived there. (Photo courtesy of the Sheridan family).

[Jim]: It was a very popular place for my mother's family to visit because those people were all from Chicago and I don't think ever had another opportunity to visit a place like this. There was one period of time when just about half her relatives that she had, which were a large number, visited all at one time. . . . My aunts and uncles who came and visited us thought that this was the greatest thing that ever lived, to have a relative who was a lighthouse keeper. And they were just as happy as larks to come. And particularly in a nice summer resort place like Saugatuck was in those days.

My aunts and uncles who came and visited us thought that this was the greatest thing . . . to have a relative who was a lighthouse keeper.

Despite the long walk to town, the Sheridans did participate in activities such as community organizations.

[George]: I know one thing my mother did. I don't know if she belonged to the Order of the Eastern Star when she lived in Chicago or not, but I know she did here [in Saugatuck] because my dad had built a rock garden in the shape of a star in the front yard of the lighthouse with rocks. And they had a rock garden there. And she talked about her going back and forth to her meetings at the Star and going through the woods at night with a lantern. And, of course, she was active in the Star for many, many years after [living at the lighthouse].

As for other kinds of gardens, Jim recalls:

No, this was an absolutely impossible thing to do there because it was [a] completely sand area. All sand. No tillable ground whatsoever. There was a heavily wooded area across the river from the lighthouse, but even that was not suitable for any--the only thing it would grow was pine trees. So, even if we had wanted to have a garden, (which we probably did, because everyone had gardens in those days), we had none.

Obtaining some kinds of fresh foods was often difficult.

[Jim]: Because we had to walk two or three miles to town, we didn't go to the store very often. Mostly, we would get a stock of vegetables and keep them in the cellar which was provided. For milk, we drank condensed milk, canned milk, evaporated milk. And as a result of the fact that I drank evaporated milk, or used it on my corn flakes or my oatmeal, I never had an opportunity to develop a liking for milk. And to this day I don't care for milk.

Their father's day to day duties at the lighthouse kept him quite busy.

[Jim]: Well, like most lighthouse keepers, there were a few things that were absolutely necessary for him to do every day. And that would be take care of the light, certainly. The light was, actually, only an oil lamp. He brought it down out of the tower each day and polished it, whether it needed it or not.

And he filled it, trimmed the wick, and put it back up there in preparation for relighting. He had to climb up into the tower through a ladder which led through it. And he also had to keep everything in order in the tower as well as the lighthouse proper.

Things that I remember mostly about his duties were, there seemed to always be a paintbrush in his hand. . . . The government put great stock in painting. They painted and they repainted and they painted, until paint usually built up so it had so many coats there were no sharp edges at all anywhere. Not such a thing as a sharp edge in any corner of a piece of wood. It always had a curved edge.

. . . there seemed to always be a paintbrush in his hand.

. . . He particularly wore the uniform on special days. When the inspector came, certainly, when he had visitors, or expected visitors, he would wear it. I remember it very well. And he had to buy his own uniforms, by the way. The government didn't supply it. . . . He also wore a white suit which he used when he did painting or cleaning or working. And I still have the middy that went with that bit of uniform--was sort of like a sailor's middy--and white trousers that went with it. I can remember him wearing that particularly around the house. And, of course, he was around the house all the time.

Occasionally a keeper helped rescue stranded boaters. Jim recalls one such incident.

My father did take part in a rescue of a yacht that came ashore, I think about 1914. It came in and ran up on the beach and he went out into the water and waded out there and carried ashore the wife and daughter of the yacht people. The man who was in the yacht, the father, got himself ashore. And strangely enough, though, the people who were in that affair became close friends of ours for the rest of our lives.

The story of how Aaron and Julia Sheridan became lighthouse keepers--and of how they came to their tragic deaths--is part of the Sheridan family's folklore.

[Jim]: My grandfather and grandmother were lighthouse keepers. . . . She was made a lighthouse keeper after they were assigned to the lighthouse at South Manitou Island. . . . Aaron Sheridan was a Civil War veteran. He fought in several battles of the Civil War including the battle of Shiloh and the battle of Chickamauga. And after the battle of Chickamauga, he was in an outfit, a regiment, that gave chase to the Confederates as they were retreating from the battle of Missionary Ridge. He received a wound in his arm about a year before the war ended . . . in the battle of Ringgold. And it was a severe wound. He had a Minie Ball hit him in the elbow and [it] destroyed his elbow. And he had the arm amputated in the field and it did not heal very well. He was put in several hospitals including one in Washington, D.C. where he stayed the rest of the war. And he got out of the hospital after the war was over and by then, it was 1866.

He then went back to Illinois where he had come from, because he lived in a little town called Yorkville, or at least he lived near there. He probably was a farmer, although, I don't know that for sure. And, of course, at that time he only had one arm. One-armed farmers were not so handy around the barn, so he evidently cast around for another job. And he was in communication with one of his cousins who were Lyman and Newton. These men were aware of the fact that the lighthouse keeper on South Manitou Island had left his position and there was a vacancy. Now, I don't know this for an absolute fact, but putting two and two together, it looks like, because of this vacancy, he was notified it was available. And he did not have any background as a sailor or a lighthouse keeper, but he applied for the job and mainly due to the fact that he was a war veteran and had lost an arm, he received the job. So, he went to South Manitou Island and spent all his years there until 1878. He was there from 1866 to 1878. Twelve years.

And at that time, he and his wife, very unfortunately, were drowned in a boating accident. They were coming back from the mainland. A squall came up, tipped over their boat, and his wife [and one year old son Robert] . . . and himself were drowned, and their bodies were never recovered. His [remaining five] children, which my father was one, then were taken back to Illinois to live with their grandparents. And they lived there throughout their youth and eventually grew up and performed other duties. None of them ever went into the Lighthouse Service except for my father.

After their father's death in 1915, the Sheridans moved to a house in Saugatuck. The lighthouse closed and in the 1950s was destroyed by a tornado.

[George]: There was really no place else to go. My dad had died, and my mother, of course, all her family lived in Chicago. The only thing left to do was to come back to Saugatuck and make the best of it. And that's where she rented this house.

And she took washings for many years to bring up the kids. And we didn't have any other income. . . . I think about 1945 or '50, the government approved an income for widows of lighthouse keepers who had not remarried. So, I think that about in 1950 she started to get a pension from the government. She didn't get any kind of a pension until that

---

The grandchildren always got a big kick out of her. They just worshipped Grandma because she was a lightkeeper's wife and they just thought that was wonderful.

---

time. So, she sent all of us three kids through college. And the only money she had was what we gave her and what she got through the government. . . . The grandchildren always got a big kick out of her. They just worshipped Grandma because she was a lightkeeper's wife and they just thought that was wonderful.

In her home in Riverview, Michigan, Dorotha Dodge relaxes among her photographs and family memorabilia while being interviewed in August 1985.
(Photo by LuAnne Gaykowski Kozma).

Dorotha Dodge

Dorotha (Story) Dodge was nearing her 84th birthday at the time of this interview on August 3, 1985. She was born in 1901 at the Mamajuda lighthouse which once stood on an island in the Detroit River. Both the lighthouse and the island no longer exist. Her father, James Townsend Story, was keeper there until 1910, when he transferred to Grosse Ile, another island light station further downriver. Near the end of her father's lighthouse career, the Story family moved again to Windmill Point light station on Lake St. Clair. Dorotha has many fond memories of her childhood at the two Detroit River island lights, and often reconstructs dialogue in her stories.   She now lives in Riverview, Michigan.

(Interviewer: LuAnne Gaykowski Kozma).

Because she was much younger than her older siblings, Dorotha was raised as an only child on Mamajuda. No other people except the Story family lived on the island. Dorotha's playmates were her pet dogs and chicken, "Chichi."

Right up until then [going to school] I had no one to play with. I just had my two dogs. And, of course, every Christmas I got a doll, but I didn't want to play with a doll. My sister's youngsters used to come over and they'd take it and they'd break them and that would be the end of them. I'd take the clothes off and put [them] on my dog.

Then I had a pet chicken, and, of course, I thought quite a lot of that pet Chichi. But, it was something alive, see. . . . I used to have my Chichi up on the table. She sat in my high chair. . . It was a bandy. And you know, she would not touch a thing on that tray until I told her she could? No, no. And that would kind of get my dad and Mama, you know, they'd talk about it. "Well, why don't you let Chichi eat?" or something, you know. [laughing] I can remember them saying that. Oh, I thought quite a lot of my Chichi, I'll tell you that.

At age eight, Dorotha attended school across the river in Wyandotte, Michigan. Getting to school by rowboat was difficult, at best.

Well, it was a mile over from Mammyjudy to Wyandotte, and Daddy would row it over there, take me to--Had to go by boat. And then I walked up to Garfield School, which wasn't too far. . . . But I didn't start school until when I was eight because Daddy, I guess, thought I was a little bit too young to go up alone and they couldn't always take me. But he would always take the boat, of course. . . .

But one time, Daddy came and got me from school and, oh, the wind was blowing just something *terrible*. So, one of the fellows there where Daddy used to--Dave Perry--where we used to dock the boat, he said, "You better not go, Jim." "Oh," he says, "I gotta go." He says, "Stella's over there all alone." And, of course, we couldn't leave the lighthouse alone, you see.

And, so, we went across the Wyandotte channel and that was a rascal. The water came right over the boat. Daddy would row, you know, and he'd say, "Babe, keep a-bailing! Keep a-bailing, Babe! Don't let it--give up!"

And, of course, we couldn't leave the lighthouse alone . . .

When we got across the Wyandotte channel, well, then it wasn't quite so bad, when we got into the river. Then we was kind of relieved. But I know Mama was--I can see her yet, standing at the dock there and wondering, you know, watching. See if we were safe or not. Well, we got home safe. If it hadn't been that we had to get home, we probably would of stayed in Wyandotte, but Daddy couldn't leave Mama over there alone.

At no time could the Story family leave the Mamajuda station unattended, not even for an occasional outing.

And then every year, of course, Daddy couldn't go, but Mama would always take me to Put-In-Bay, Boblo, or we'd go on the TASHMOO up to Port Huron. There'd be one of them that we would go on. Sometimes we used to go twice. . . . Just for an excursion, you know, just like they do now. And, oh, I thought that was just fine. Of course, I guess Mama must have enjoyed it because she'd always go, but Daddy never went. He couldn't! He had to stay on. Just couldn't.

In winter, they rented an apartment on the mainland so young Dorotha could attend school more easily.

And then when I went to school to Wyandotte--I lived in Mammyjudy--Mama and I would go over and rent a apartment. We used to have another fellow by the name of Gordon Small. I remember him. And Daddy used to hire him to stay at the lighthouse. We didn't have the light a-going. But somebody had to be at the building all the time. . . . Then [Daddy] would come and stay with us in the apartment, see. But he didn't do it very often. Oh, maybe, about a couple of weeks or something like that. And then he'd go back. Well, he went practically two or three times a week back to see everything was all right. And not only that, but take supplies over to Gordon. . . . Well, after [winter] we would move back and then Daddy would take me back and forth then.

For the Story family, keeping the light was a shared responsibility.

Oh, yes, [Mama] knew how to take care of it. Then I didn't know how to take care of it till we went to Grosse Ile and I was old enough to know then. So, I used to go up and help him put the light up, the lamp up, into the great big, oh, I don't know what you would call it, container, anyway. And that would revolve, you see, would keep a-going round and round.

. . . After Mama passed away, why, Daddy was quite ill. So, he was in bed. The doctor put him in bed. And, so, I used to go up--my aunt come and lived with us so that she could help take [care of] Daddy--but I went up the tower to the beacon and I'd *run* up those steps! And I know one time, my aunt says, "I'm gonna follow you!" And every time I start running she'd

*A postcard depicting the Mamajuda lighthouse on the Detroit
River prior to 1911. The Story family lived there from circa
1899 to circa 1910. (Courtesy of the Van Hoey Collection).*

follow in back! . . . Well, she was worried, you know,
something would happen. She says, "You're doing that too
fast." But I got the light up there anyway!

**When she grew older, Dorotha helped her father with
other chores at the Grosse Ile station, including
painting.**

He would have me paint, go up the towers, you know, or
skeleton, whatever you call them things. And I'd have to paint
there, helping. Of course, when I was in school there I was
only seventeen, no, sixteen it was. And I wore my dad's
overalls, you know. And I was out there painting and I seen
the Navy. (It was during the war at this time, First World
War. And the Navy landed at Grosse Ile. This was all on
Grosse Ile). And the captain and, oh, a couple of the fellows
came, and I seen 'em coming. And I told my dad, I said, "Get
me down on the ground." I said, "I've got to go to the
bathroom." And he said, "All right." That was my excuse. I
sneaked behind the boathouse 'cause I didn't want the boys to
see *me!* [pauses] So, they asked where I was. My dad said,
"In there." [pauses] My dad got it afterwards! [laughing] Of
course, they found me, you know. And here I had these
overalls on. [It] was just embarrassing. I'll never forget that, I
don't think.

**On at least one occasion, Dorotha was responsible for
the light at Grosse Ile while her father was away.
Although her older sister helped her, she remembers
how difficult it was to keep the light burning properly.**

Daddy went to visit his relatives in Seneca Falls, New York. And, of course, I had to take care of the light. So, we [Dorotha and her sister] went up, got this light all right. And the beacon, some way or other I had done--and it smoked. Well, Daddy was reported because some ship reported. Well,

---

Well, the next morning we got a telephone call: "What was the matter with the light, the beacon light?"

---

the next morning we got a telephone call: "What was the matter with the light, the beacon light?" Didn't know. And I went up early in the morning and changed it! But I didn't think it was anything wrong with it. So, I went back. I told my sister, I says, "I wonder why that light didn't light." And, so I went back. Come to find out I had a smokehouse. It was funny, I had my mind on taking that down and cleaning the lamp and everything and put it right where it was supposed to be. I never thought of looking up in the ceiling, see, all the smoke. 'Cause the light was out.

Well, the next night I said to my sister, I said, "Well, we're going to go up there. We'll go in the boat. We'll take the boat out, and we'll row up. And then we'll come back and see what's the matter with that light."

Sure enough, we had another smokehouse. And I thought, "Oh, something wrong." My sister said, "Where's those other

Dorotha Dodge and her father, keeper James Story, in circa 1913. (Photo courtesy of Dorotha Dodge).

lamps?" And I said, "There they are." She says, "Get some oil in there. We're going to fix that." Something I had done, see--that I *didn't* do. And, well, the next morning I had to go up and wash the ceiling and everything again. But, Daddy wasn't reported the second time 'cause we took care of that! [laughs] But see, funny, now this one here, I got along just fine. That was Grosse Ile, that happened.

So, when Daddy came home, that was the first thing I told him. And he says, "Well, what happened?" I said, "I don't know!" So, that night, he went up with me. And he says, "We'll find out what happened." We went up there. Some little thing inside the lamp that I hadn't put down right. Because I left it just the way we took it out, see. And he says, "Here it is, Babe. How did you ever happen to not *notice* that?" I said, "I don't know." He said, "Did you take that out and clean it, [the way] I showed you?" I said, "Yes, I-did." [laughing:] But I didn't put it back, snap it down! Well, anyway, he said, "Well, that's all right," he said. But, the report wasn't very bad anyway, so, they didn't say anything to Dad. I was scared stiff, though. I thought sure that some[thing] would happen. And, of course, the people on Grosse Ile knew that I was there to take care of it. My sister was with me. She lived with me while Daddy was gone. He was gone about two weeks. And she went and took care of that lamp after that! [laughing:] I wouldn't! I thought, "If you get it wrong, well, it'll be your fault, not mine." Because she knew how to do it. She'd done it before.

*In the above photograph taken circa 1904 entitled "Home of a
Lighthouse-Keeper," young Ralph Warner and his sisters
Margaret, Bessie, and Isabell row a boat in front of the
family's dwelling in Sault Ste. Marie, Michigan. Their
grandmother is on the porch. (Copyright ©1904 by Harper's
Magazine. All rights reserved. Reprinted from the April issue
by special permission).*

Ralph Warner

*Born in Sault Ste. Marie, Michigan, in 1896, Ralph
James Warner was one of four children of Fred and
Christine Warner. After their mother's death in 1903,
Ralph and his sisters lived with relatives during most of
the year and with their father, who kept several lights
along the St. Mary's River, during the summers. Ralph
was interviewed in Harrisville, Michigan, on April 27,
1985 at the age of 89. He passed away in August
1985.*

(Interviewer: Richard Moehl; Indexer: Brenda Marr).

Fred Warner, he was a operator at a lighthouse at the "Soo."
He had one lighthouse at the bridge where it went across to
Canada, and one where the boats come in the river on the
canal. . . . It was right on the point of the canal where it comes
into the Soo Locks. . . . We lived in a shack at the end of the
bridge that goes across to Canada. . . . My dad had to get up
different times in the night and make sure that [the lights] were
on. He had one on the end of the canal and one on the bridge
going across Canada.

Well, of course, I was only a kid, eight years old then, and I
didn't know much about it. I used to run up and down the
circular stairway, up the lighthouse, and all that kind of stuff,
you know.

Living at a Lighthouse

Ralph Warner's life at a lighthouse has been noted in print once before, when he was a small boy. Keeper Fred Warner and his four children caught the attention of Louise Morgan Sill while she was on an excursion through the Great Lakes. Writing about her trip for the April 1904 issue of *Harper's Monthly Magazine* in an article entitled "Through Inland Seas," Sill described the Warner family and their dwelling. She took particular notice of young Ralph:

> "At the edge of the town we found a small bit of Holland--a house, a strip of garden, a pond large enough for one boat to turn around in without grazing the shore, a cow and chickens, and four flaxen-haired children as reigning lords of this Lilliputian domain. Their father was one of the many lighthouse-keepers we met, and a cheerful grandmother cared for the motherless children. To get the children and the cow in proper position for the picture was a work of rare finesse; but when it was finally arranged, the little boy was more interested in the correct attitude of the cow than in his own, of which misplaced concern on his part the picture bears evidence."

Ralph has his own story about the *Harper's Monthly* photograph (see page 44):

This ladder, you can see here, the old man had to have that ladder up there because this is a stovepipe coming through the roof there. Now, in the winter time it'd catch fire, you know, the tar-paper roof, catch on fire. The old man would have to go out and chop a hole in the ice and go up that ladder there and put the fire out.

Seemed like he was always busy at the lighthouse doing different things. You got to clean up the lights and keep them cleaned up and keep the lighthouse painted up and all that kind of stuff, you know. So, he was kept pretty busy at the lighthouse . . .

Recalling that his father associated with another keeper in the area, he pointed out that the two keepers occasionally helped each other at their light stations.

There was another lighthouse keeper up the river, seems to me it was further up the river or down the river, by the name of Sweet that my dad chummed around with quite a bit. Him and this Sweet got along pretty good together on situations, you know, that they had at the lighthouse. They had to keep the lighthouses clean, keep 'em painted up and all that kind of stuff, you know.

Walking a long way to school is often remembered as a
difficult experience, but for the Warner children it was
especially frightening.

Well, I remember when my sister, my oldest sister Margaret,
and I got started at school we had to cross the locks, you
know. We lived on the rapids side of the locks, see. And we
had to cross the locks in order to get up to the schoolhouse that
stood up on a kind of a knoll. . . . And we had to cross on our
hands and knees sometimes on those locks because one of
them that didn't have any rail on, ([some] had a hand railing so
you could hang on to something), because the wind got
blowing pretty hard down that canal. So, lots of times we'd
have to crawl on our hands and knees across the locks that
didn't have any rail on.

The Warner family obtained some of their food from the
water and land around them. Ralph did his part to help
the family.

We ate mostly fish, you know. That was the easiest food to
get. . . . Of course, my dad had a launch, you know, with an
inboard motor instead of an outboard motor. And we had a
boathouse. We kept the boat in the boathouse most of the time.
. . . [The boathouse was] right at the lighthouse residence,
where the lighthouse was. And I used to lay on my stomach
and catch fish in the boathouse, you know, 'cause I could see
'em--clear water down there--and I was always trying to get a
hook in front of them, you know, so I could catch one. . . .
And first thing you know, I'd be going "bunk" down in the
hole! Fall in. But the water wasn't very deep.

We bought most of our vegetables. We did have a little garden that we raised some vegetables in, but we had to buy some. Potatoes and stuff like that that we didn't raise, you know, 'cause we didn't have much land. And, of course, my dad didn't have too much time of having a garden.

We ate mostly fish, you know. That was the easiest food to get.

. . . Seemed like he was always busy at the lighthouse doing different things. You got to clean up the lights and keep them cleaned up and keep the lighthouse painted up and all that kind of stuff, you know. So, he was kept pretty busy at the lighthouse, I would say. . . . I didn't have much to do. Only fish.

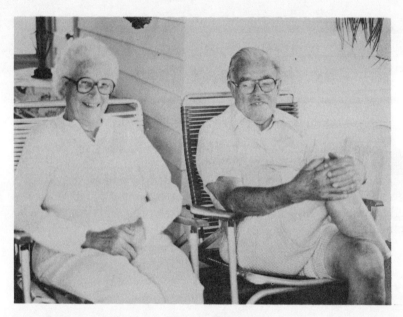

Loretta Pearson and her husband, Arthur, at their home in Grand Rapids, Michigan, on July 22, 1985. (Photo by Karen McDonnell-Dziesinski).

Loretta Pearson

Loretta (Bush) Pearson lived at the White River light station on Lake Michigan near Whitehall, Michigan, until she was fourteen years old. Her great-grandfather, William Robinson, was a keeper there for over forty years. Her father, William Bush, succeeded him, serving as assistant keeper and keeper at White River for nearly thirty years. Loretta was interviewed on July 22, 1985 by the curator of White River Light Station, which is now operated as a museum. She currently lives in Grand Rapids, Michigan.

(Interviewer: Karen McDonnell-Dziesinski; Transcriber: Lois Mason)

In 1910, when Loretta was a small child, her family moved in with her elderly great-grandfather, Captain William Robinson, at the White River lighthouse.

Well, we moved in with Great-Grandpa Robinson, who was the keeper at that time. His family was all gone. He needed someone to keep house for him. So, my father talked my mother into coming in there and being a housekeeper for him. We were just small children when we moved in there.

Although having the family to help with chores made things easier for Captain Robinson, the sudden addition of small children must have been somewhat disruptive.

Well, he was very gruff. He was kind and he loved us children. I used to write letters for him to his sons and daughters when I got old enough to do that. But at the same time, when we were little children we bothered him and in the evening after we'd have our dinner, we'd have to stay in the kitchen. And if we laughed--you know how children do laugh and talk--he'd shut the door and he'd tell us to shut our loud mouths [laughing]. But, it was just his way of talking. And when the work was done in the kitchen we went upstairs and we played games upstairs in the bedroom. We couldn't be down where he was. It bothered him. But he was an old man, so, we didn't think anything of it.

When Captain Robinson retired, his grandson, Loretta's father, became the keeper and worked there until the early 1940s.

He had to tend the lights and keep the lights. When he first started there were kerosene lamps there. And those lamps had to be polished every day. He had to keep the windows clean on the tower. . . . Also, there was the light on the pier at that time that had a kerosene lamp that had to be lit every night and extinguished in the morning. He also had a small foghorn. When the fishermen would go out, if it was foggy, he'd stand on the pier and crank a horn to make the old foghorn go, and help them. When we used to be small children, the Goodrich boats used to come in from Chicago and carried the passengers over to the resort area. If it was a foggy day when they came in, he would do the same for them.

Besides operating the light and foghorn, Loretta's father was responsible for maintaining the grounds. Inspectors visited regularly to ensure that the keeper was performing the required duties.

He had to keep the yard grass cut and the place clean, inside and out. We never knew when the government men were coming. They would come and inspect. They'd go right straight through your house, open closet doors and everything. If things weren't in order you got a demerit mark for it.

We never knew when the government men were coming.

Loretta recalls the circumstances of the one and only time her father received a demerit from an inspector.

My mother was ill and he'd taken her to Whitehall to the doctor. We children were left to do dishes and we left a frying pan on the stove. He got a demerit mark because that frying pan was on the stove.

Certain chores were required to be finished by a specific time of day. Sometimes, this caused a hardship for the Bush family.

. . . The laundry was not supposed to be on the line after

eleven in the morning. . . . That's the only thing I remember, the laundry on the line. And that was hard to do because my mother rubbed the clothes on the old rub board. With a family of three children and three adults--there was Grandpa's clothing, too--it took her quite a while to do it, and you don't always have nice weather up there around the lake. Breezes don't always blow and dry the clothes the way they should. It's different today with the automatics.

The inspectors came about twice a year and the family always had to be prepared because no one ever knew when those visits would occur. Sometimes, though, they would receive advance notice.

Well, I'll tell you, these kind of work together. If [the inspectors] stop at the Muskegon station first, [the Muskegon station would] call, or the other way around. Kind of warn you. That's how they got caught the one time I told you that we left the frying pan on the stove. He'd taken my mother to the doctor and he didn't get the warning. But, when we knew [the inspectors] were coming, we called up there and he came back, but it was too late. And we kids didn't think about taking that old frying pan off the stove.

Loretta recalls that her father always wore the same uniform, summer and winter, although in the warmer months he sometimes went without the coat.

I know he used to wear blue shirts all the time. And he was supposed to wear a tie when he was dressed fully, you know. But unless he thought it was an inspector coming especially in the summer months, he kind of left his collar open.

Loretta's mother took care of the house, cooked, and cleaned for both Captain Robinson and her own family. Sometimes she assisted her husband with his duties.

After I was gone from there, my father had a blood clot in his leg and he was confined to bed for ten days. While he was in bed she took care of the light in the tower. At that time they had the automatic light on the pier, so, she didn't have that work. But she did take care of the one in the tower on the house.

Modernization did not necessarily mean less work for a lighthouse keeper. The electric light was not always reliable, so, Loretta's father continued to maintain the old kerosene system as a back-up.

I don't know how it is up there now, but it used to be if you had a little storm the electricity went out and then if it didn't come on soon, he'd have to disassemble [the electric light] and put the kerosene lamp in there.

There was ample time for recreation, especially for the children.

We used to play on the beach a lot. In the summer months we went swimming every day. When we were small, my mother went to the beach with us. I don't know what good it would have done because she couldn't swim a stroke, but she went to watch us to make sure we were all right. So, we played on the beach that way. But, other than that, we stayed in the yard.

Social life revolved around visiting with family and
friends; occasionally there were picnics and dances.

There was the Murrays at the hotel down there. They lived
there the year around. And then there was the Andersons; they
were caretakers of the resort area. And then, of course, when
the Coast Guard [station] was active, there were all the families
across the channel. And they all had families that lived there,
and so they were all, you might say, neighbors.

. . . My mother and her sister married brothers and so they
were back and forth a lot. My aunt and uncle lived about a mile
from my folks--from the lighthouse. Well, a week to ten days,
maybe every two weeks, we'd get together. When we were
children, we walked. We thought nothing of walking that mile
back and forth to see each other. And another thing, my father
had a nice row boat and he liked to row. And sometimes he'd
row us over . . . where they were living. So, we saw each
other real often and we all went to school together.

[There were] never any picnics except our school picnic. My
mother would always go to that. We always had a school
picnic in the spring. They used to have square dances and
things like that they used to go to once in a while in the winter
months. Later on, after I was gone from out that area,
resorters liked to square dance and there was one family that
used to have them every week. Did it commercially, you
know. But my folks didn't go to that. They used to go and,
just with their friends, have coffee clutches they called them.
Just sit and visit and have a cup of coffee and something sweet
to eat with it.

Usually, the family walked to town, but there were some

alternative modes of transportation.

My father was a good skater and when White Lake was frozen over he would skate to town. He had a sled with a handle on the back end of it and he put a box or chair or something on there for my mother, if she wanted to go to town, and skate her up to town. But as children, we never got to town unless we had a toothache or something. And then we would go with somebody else that had horses. They'd take us. But other than that, as a family, we walked because, like I say, we didn't have any transportation. . . .When we were small, before people had too many cars, there were what they call ferry boats. They used to stop at all the resort areas. And you could ride, during the summer months, from down at the lake there clear up to Whitehall and Montague. They would stop all along, take people. There were three or four different owners that had these boats. So, you had transportation that way in the summer months. But it was winter when we didn't have anything, only what we would do for ourselves.

Loretta looks back on living at the lighthouse and what she believes her father found most enjoyable about his job:

I think that living there. It was a beautiful spot. In the summer months when the resorters were around, they used to come up there [to the lighthouse] and he used to get a chance to visit with them. They'd come up every night and look at the sunset and things like that and I think that made it pleasant for him.

Marie Hering with her husband, Robert, in their Whitewater, Wisconsin home in fall, 1985. (Photo by Jean D. Gertz).

Marie Hering

Marie (Bevry) Hering grew up at two Wisconsin lighthouses--Wind Point and Pilot Island--on Lake Michigan and was married at the Wind Point light station. Her father, Henry Bevry, worked in the U. S. Lighthouse Service starting in 1899 and retired at age seventy in 1944. Marie was interviewed at her home in Whitewater, Wisconsin, on September 20 and October 25, 1985.

(Interviewer: Jean D. Gertz).

Marie's father first worked in the Lighthouse Service at Cana Island lighthouse, off Wisconsin's Door Peninsula, which Marie affectionately calls "Caney Island." As he continued his career and transferred to other stations--Pilot Island and Wind Point--his family grew. By about 1912, the Bevrys moved again to Wind Point lighthouse near Racine, Wisconsin, where Mr. Bevry served as keeper for 32 years.

He started in the year he was married in 1899 and he was at Caney Island there. And he probably was there about three years. . . . While there, their first child, Grace, was born. Then he was sent to Wind Point as an assistant and while there, they had a son and a daughter. . . . Then he was transferred to Pilot [Island lighthouse] . . . I was born after they were at Pilot. And, as I mentioned, the women and children could not stand the winter months on Pilot because of the severe weather,

and sometimes it was completely iced over, and so, my
mother, with the three children, was living on Washington
Island when I was born . . . in December of 1908. And he
remained at Pilot Island until I was four years old. So, he must
have moved to Wind Point [the second time] about 1912. . . .
My brother, Donald, and sister, Dorothy, were actually born at
Wind Point lighthouse.

**The family's years at the more isolated stations, Pilot
Island and Cana Island, Marie suspects were difficult
for her mother.**

. . . Of course she went to Caney Island as a bride of nineteen.
And then, they couldn't live in the lighthouse because the
keeper's family was too large. . . . I think she might have had
some scary nights when Dad was on duty over there when she
was alone.

**While living at Pilot Island, transportation during the
winters was hazardous. Marie tells of an incident
when her father miraculously survived a winter trip on
foot.**

I know my dad mentioned that one year, he and one of the men
were skating in from Pilot to Washington and he fell through
the ice! And he couldn't get up because of the heavy clothing
and the skates on. The ice kept breaking and he just couldn't
get up and he thought sure he was a goner. But the man with
him went to shore and got a long branch of a tree or something
and was able push it out to him that he could hang onto it, and
he pulled him out. And he continued on to Washington Island.
And the clothes had frozen on him that he was a sheet of ice;

that he wasn't even cold inside. He didn't even catch cold from it.

Moving back to Wind Point lighthouse made it easier on the whole family. The town of Racine, neighbors, schools, and stores were much closer.

When we moved, Dad had gone on to Racine ahead of the family, and the lighthouse boat--I think it probably was the SUMAC--moved Mother and all our furniture and the kids right to Wind Point.

. . . the lighthouse boat . . . moved Mother and all our furniture and the kids right to Wind Point.

. . . You see, we were in a farm community. We weren't like on an island or anything . . . so that there were other families nearby that had children that you could go to play with or they could come down to play with you. . . . Up there [at Pilot Island], it was mostly your lighthouse families, where here [at Wind Point], you were in a community.

. . . In the early days, at that time [circa 1913], none of us had a car and it was four miles into town. There were grocery stores that would deliver to you. But we, in the summertime, used to go to town with our launch, the government launch. And the water at that time was deep enough to do that and we would go to town. Whatever man had that afternoon off would go to town, maybe bring home the groceries for the other two families if they couldn't go. Or if the women could go they would go along. They would tie up the boat at the Main Street bridge and it was just a few blocks to the downtown area in Racine, and they could do grocery shopping, they could take in a show, and then meet there to go home again. . . . They couldn't do it in the winter because it would get too bad. Then they used to walk . . . till later on, when they came to buy cars.

At Wind Point lighthouse, Mr. Bevry received certificates for a well-maintained station. Marie recalls that inspections and off-duty afternoons were times when the men would wear the official uniforms.

They didn't wear [uniforms] when they were working. In fact, a lot of their work was, you know, if they were shoveling coal or painting and that, you couldn't wear a uniform. But in the afternoon, if you were off duty, my dad, himself--and liked his men to--kind of dress up. And, of course, if they knew the inspector was coming, then they all put their uniforms on. . . . Oh, you bet your life [they knew an inspector was coming] because they would call from downtown and let you know!

. . . They did keep the place immaculate. Every spring, if there were painting to do, they would do it, and I think that the tower was whitewashed every year. And the men did that themselves and, of course, they kept the light in perfect condition. All the brass and all the glass was always polished. 'Cause you never knew when the inspector was coming.

The sound of the foghorn at Wind Point was very loud. But in general, the keepers' families--and most people

living in the vicinity--did not mind the noise.

Well, I think that most of the neighbors had been there so long they were quite accustomed to it, as we were. We wouldn't even wake up when it started. But in later years, when some of the farms had been sold and there were some rather wealthy people that were buying up farm land out there, . . . one of them called down after the first time that she had heard it start, wanting to know if [we] would please notify her ahead of time or if they could start it "more gently."

But, as far as the foghorn, we didn't pay any attention to it.

. . . But, as far as the foghorn, we didn't pay any attention to it. But after I was married and would bring the children out there to visit, they didn't like it at all, and neither did my little nephew. My mother would try to tell him that it had to be, because the ships that were going on the lake needed it because it was foggy. And he says, "That's okay, turn it off anyway."

Joe St. Andre stands in front of his childhood home, the Keweenaw Waterway Lower Entry light station, in the Keweenaw Peninsula of Michigan in October 1985. Today, he lives near the light station in the Bootjack area of Lake Linden. (Photo by Tom Kozma).

Joseph St. Andre

Joseph St. Andre has known many Great Lakes lighthouses. He was born in 1908 at the Tawas Point light station on Lake Huron where his father, Oliver St. Andre, was keeper. His grandfather had been a keeper at Seul Choix Point lighthouse. With his twelve brothers and sisters, Joe was raised at the Marquette light station from 1912 to 1916 and then at the Keweenaw Waterway Lower Entry light station (once called Portage Lake Lower Entry), both on Lake Superior. At age sixteen he joined the U.S. Lighthouse Service and for twelve years served on a construction crew, working at numerous lighthouses throughout lakes Superior, Huron, and Erie during most months of the year and repairing lighthouse tenders and lightships in Detroit during the winter. The interview took place on October 25, 1985 at his Lake Linden, Michigan home, and on the grounds of the Keweenaw Waterway Lower Entry light station.

(Interviewer: LuAnne Gaykowski Kozma).

Joe remembers the strict inspections by the U. S. Lighthouse Service officials and his family's rush to prepare the house.

And then, at each year, about middle of the summer, an inspector came. . . .Yes, that was quite a thing to get ready for that. See, in them days we didn't have the advance information. You *knew* where he was. They tried to get word from each station so that each family would know when they [the inspectors] come.

But that inspector *was* an inspector, too. . . . Oh, you had to clean everything and you painted every three years whether it needed it or not. They'd chip it off, take it off, and paint again. And when that man [the inspector] came, well, he was like probably the "second coming of the Lord" or something. I don't know, that's putting it kind of rough, but he'd come there and, well, we'd all hide or whatever. Sweep everything under the rug as quick as you could if you could, so that he'd come in--But he'd walk in, he'd go right upstairs, through all the rooms, go into the bedrooms. It is said, now, I do not know whether it's true, but, the man had gloves on, and he'd go up and rub across the chest of drawers or whatever you had up there, to see if there was any dust on it. I'd never seen him do that, but some people said he did.

Discipline and manners were important to the St. Andre family--especially around the dinner table. Joe recalls his family's mealtime customs and his parents' chidings:

The law was laid down to us, as far as eating was concerned, with that family because Dad said that "This is no restaurant." And he said, "Breakfast will be at six o'clock, dinner at noon . . . and supper"--you know, that was the three meals--"at six." Now, if the dishes are being cleared away before you get there, you do not get nothing to eat until the next meal. We never ate between meals. . . . So, you were there on time.

. . . You came to *eat*. "This is no place for conversation."
When you were at the table, you came there to eat. You eat, eat
slowly, and chew your food good. "There'll be no talking,"
because, again, "This is no restaurant. Mother has a lot of
work to do." . . . Oh, we did [talk] later years, we would, you
know. But while we were young, we were--And whatever
you take on your plate you *eat*. You *do* not leave anything on
there. And if the plate comes around to you, why, you *don't*
take the biggest piece. You take the middle size or the small
one, as it goes around. So, you can plainly see why, like I
alway said, you know, when the people talking about a big
family--I was about in the middle of the family--and I said, "I
was twenty-one years old before I knew there was anything but
a wing and a neck on a chicken."

*But, every Sunday morning he
would lead us all upstairs into
their bedroom and we'd have to
say the rosary. . . . We couldn't
get to church.*

Being far away from a church, the St. Andre family
sometimes had to improvise.

One of the things I recall--Dad was a very religious man. He
was a Catholic, see, very religious. And when we moved
down here [to Keweenaw Waterway Lower Entry], well, you
couldn't go to church. And he was *bound* that we would go to

church on Sunday, you know, whenever there was a church available. But, every Sunday morning he would lead us all upstairs into their bedroom and we'd have to say the rosary. . . .We couldn't get to church. But he said, "If you don't go to church you've got to do something." So, he'd go up there and he'd lead us all in the rosary. We'd all have to kneel down and . . . we had to say the rosary every Sunday morning. It didn't make any difference who was there. They didn't have to go with us, but he'd excuse us and line us up, saying the rosary.

Besides playing cards in the evenings, the St. Andre family spent a lot of their time reading. Books were provided by the U. S. Lighthouse Service.

The Lighthouse Service had lending libraries. There was a box about, oh, I'm going to say probably three feet square and probably eighteen inches deep. And, them boats would take that library from one station to another one. You had no choice of what library you were to get. They just gave it to you. But that was full of books for reading. They were good books. But every time we'd get a library we'd start reading a book and everybody'd grab a book and sit in the corner and read. But you didn't want to take somebody's placemarker out of it, or that was criminal. . . . Sometimes you'd say, "Give me it when you're through with it, or halfway through with it. I want that book." But that lighthouse department did give you these lending libraries. I've never seen any more. They had open doors on the front. . . . They were made out of oak. They were a heavy-made piece of equipment. Well, every lighthouse had them. I don't know where they originated from. That is, [there] didn't seem to be any place where they stored or kept them. They just kept them on the move from one lighthouse to another. They'd take one away and bring another one in. Sometimes you'd have two of 'em.

Living near the water was occasionally hazardous for a family with small children. While being interviewed at the Keweenaw Waterway light station grounds, Joe recounts his brother Paul's near drowning.

The only one time we ever had any trouble--[Paul] was a little guy like that--on a Sunday we came from church. (We went to church in Chassell. We took a rowboat and we went across and we had a car, and we'd go to Chassell). . . . My sister was sitting on the porch and I come out, and I was reading the Sunday paper and I told her, I said, "Where are them kids?" She said, "They're in the backyard playing." So, I said, "You better watch 'em because they're--you know, you never know, they get close to the edge of the dock, they'll fall in." "Oh," she said, "They're in the back." So, I went back in again and I started reading the paper. Something told me that there was something wrong, see. So, I come out again and I said, "Have you seen them lately?" She said, "They're in the back, playing." "I don't know." So, I walked out to here [the water]. And when I got on the edge, there was one of them in the lake. And he was going down! He was underwater. Clear, like this. I just looked over the edge and I'd seen him, you know.

I had a suit, shoes, and a tie on. I threw my coat off, kicked my shoes off, and I went after him, you know. I got him before he was down. He must have been in the water for some time. I don't know how he floated like that. But I got him. I got a hold of him and I pulled him up to the top and then I hung on and hollered for her because I couldn't get him out of the water. . . . It didn't hurt him any. But, I saved him from drowning anyway. . . . Something told me that there was something wrong, so, some way or other, I had a premonition that I had to go someplace. But, I went right straight to the spot and looked over. He was underwater about three feet. . . . But, that was the only one of the kids that ever did get in trouble. He fell off--he said he was looking at a bird or something and he went in. . . . But, we just took him home and tipped him over a little bit, . . . took him up, put him to bed, and covered him up. In a little while he was all right. He was up and around. It didn't hurt him. But he always remembered that, when I saved him from drowning. . . . You were pretty much on your own. But then, you watched them to see that they didn't go--but then everyone learned to swim. It wasn't long before they all [did].

At sixteen, Joe joined the U. S. Lighthouse Service and sent his money home to help the family.

After I got out of school in '23, I worked around for a little bit. There wasn't much doing. . . . I went to work for the lighthouse department in the fall of '25, running a boat up and down the river for a repair crew while they reconstructed these range lights and that along the river. . . . Then the next year, in '26, I went to Whitefish Point and we took all the steam--there were steam whistles in all of them. They blew by boiler. We took the boilers all out and we put air in. We also built radio towers and put radio direction finders in.

The crew went from station to station, traveling on the lighthouse tenders. Sometimes they stayed only a few weeks; other times it took several summers to complete a major construction job.

When we went to an island on construction, we took over the

whole operation. We could use [the] lighthouse keepers. We were suppose to, but we never did. Well, we always felt that he had his job to do and he worked before we got there. We didn't want to interfere. But we could have used them to help us on any job. There was, generally, about eight or ten of us. We had two or three ironworkers, two or three carpenters, an electrician, and radio man.

Living from lighthouse to lighthouse, the crew sometimes made their own, makeshift quarters.

Any time we went to a lighthouse, the lighthouse keeper had to give us quarters and food. Most of the time the quarters really wasn't what you'd have today. I cut a bunch of boughs and turned them like this and threw our blankets over 'em and that's where we slept, but, then they always gave us our meals. And each meal, they got forty-five cents a meal. I can remember that from way back. We got three meals a day there. Then we slept in the lighthouse most of the time. Some places, they were not so equipped; we slept in the oil shed there. Made ourselves a place to sleep.

The crew wintered at the U.S. Lighthouse Service depot building in Detroit.

After I left Whitefish Point, then I started working in Detroit at the foot of Mount Elliott. We had a vessel yard they called it. All the vessels would come there in the winter time. . . . Then we would go to work on them vessels and do all the repair work. That is, not the engine, but if their decks were bad, we'd tear up the decks. . . . And we repaired the AMARANTH, MARIGOLD, and also the HURON and the ST. CLAIR lightship. Both of them were tied up.

. . . Then when spring came, they'd take them away and all the vessels would go. Then we'd go out on the islands. . . . Then I worked on various jobs--Devils Island, Outer Island--oh, from year to year. But each year I'd go back to Detroit . . . And if we wanted to fabricate some of the steel for that lighthouse, . . . we did our own fabrication.

I traveled to many, many of the lighthouses on the lakes. If there is any I missed, I don't know where it was.

. . . Then we'd load it on these lighthouse tenders like the AMARANTH, ASPEN. . . . Then we'd take it to these islands and they'd unload it. We took everything out--they'd haul us out there, too, with all the boxes of tools and lumber, throw us off and leave us. And there was no going to the hardware store for a bolt or nut. You better have it with you or--[laughing] We'd complete that [job] without going to a store. Now, . . . I owned a construction company in Ann Arbor for, I don't know, eighteen years, something like that, fifteen years--but anyway, I had to be in the hardware store every day.

The St. Andres knew other lighthouse families of the area. Joe came to know many more through his travels.

Living at a Lighthouse

Well, all of us knew within, you know, a few miles of one another. I'm going to say a hundred miles or something like that. But . . . I got to know a lot of them because I traveled to many, many of the lighthouses on the lakes. If there is any I missed, I don't know where it was.

While on the porch of the keeper's dwelling, Joe recalls how he met his wife, Margaret, at the lighthouse when they were youngsters. They married in 1935. Margaret passed away in 1983.

I met her right here. Of course, I was about six or seven years older than her. She moved to the lighthouse after we did. They came sometime after we did. Maybe five or six years after we moved, they came here. . . . But I met her as a lighthouse keeper's daughter. Oh, we got chummy and for a long time we were just good friends. And then finally we got married. . . . [Her father] was the first assistant keeper. . . . Her name was Margaret McDonald. . . . We didn't get married [until] I was twenty-five, I guess. She was twenty or something like that. Nineteen? . . . Well, that's all you knew. You know lighthouse keepers and it's like the farmer's daughter, you know? You know the next farmer's daughter. Why, we could speak lighthouse language. The both of us.

Don Nelson, of Marquette, Michigan, on October 24, 1985.
(Photo by LuAnne Gaykowski Kozma).

Living at a Lighthouse

Donald L. Nelson

Don Nelson served in the U. S. Coast Guard at Keweenaw Waterway Lower Entry light station on Lake Superior for three years, from 1953 to 1955. He and his wife, Barbara, now live in Marquette, Michigan. The interview took place in the Nelsons' home on October 24, 1985.

(Interviewer: LuAnne Gaykowski Kozma).

The Keweenaw Waterway Lower Entry light station's family quarters consisted of a duplex for two families and a single-family dwelling for the officer-in-charge.

When I was there, fortunately, the bulk of the time, the three families that were there were families that seemed to enjoy the station and weren't always in a hurry as soon as they got off duty or in winter time, have to rush to get away from the station . . . This was our home. We left the station for the necessities of life such as groceries or once in a while a movie or that. But, basically, our time was spent right there. We had to get along and we did get along well at that particular station.

Although there were other lights in the Keweenaw area, the families at the station did not socialize much with families at nearby lights, as Don notes:

. . . only because your duty time never seemed to fall in with the duty time of someone that you knew at the other stations. And, naturally, on our off-duty time I think the last thing you want to do is go out and see someone else at another lighthouse. Even if you did, generally, your family had other things in mind.

And, naturally, on our off-duty time I think the last thing you want to do is go out and see someone else at another lighthouse.

. . . If we had more than two or three days time off we'd drive to Marquette, which is my hometown and where all my family and relatives were. We didn't do that too often, either. We were satisfied where we were at, there. And we enjoyed it. I can't say my feelings would have been that way if I was on some isolated island station or crib station out in the middle of the lake somewhere.

On the other hand, there was time for being neighborly with the local farmers.

There was always the local community club of Jacobsville, which was just several miles from the station. They had a local community club which was very active. . . . We participated when we weren't on duty. They had strawberry festivals in the summertime. There were get-togethers with farmers and other residents of the area. Nothing really on a scheduled basis. It was all a friendly type of thing. You got to know people. . . . We did have one local store in Jacobsville that we called "the federal building." This was a store, a post office, a gas station, and part-time auto repair garage for the area. And everyone congregated there because they had all their pigeon holes for their mail. . . . It seemed to be a central meeting place where you got to know everybody.

The families at the station spent their leisure time and holidays together in a variety of ways.

Hobbies, if you want to call them hobbies, I guess on my own it was woodcarving. Studying. There was a lot of study time, which was institute courses, and courses in my particular case on engines and that pertaining to my rate. There was a boatswain's mate by the name of Tom Cofal that built a boat there. But, basically, the rest of it was hunting, fishing, socializing. . . . card playing. Oh, yes, lots of card playing. . . . We'd spend our Christmases there. It was like any typical Christmas. We'd have a Christmas tree with the gifts for the kids. Nothing big, nothing spectacular. But, generally, there were get-togethers with the families there on the station. As I recall, we did not socialize during the Christmas or the holidays with any of the local people. So, it was strictly a station type of thing.

Other holidays were times for guests and parties.

Fourth of July, generally, were good times. As I recall, always on Fourth of July we always had good weather there the years that I was there. Generally, there would be relatives of all the fellows that were stationed there. . . . Everyone

would have friends and relatives visiting. So, there was a lot
of partying. Not much work done. But I will state that it
never affected the station as far as watch-standing. There was
a lot of partying. Lots of good food. Just amongst the families
on the station and their relatives. Because it seemed to be that
the Fourth of July was a summer break when the relatives
seemed to feel, "Hey, wouldn't it be nice to spend three or four
days down at a lighthouse?" So, we'd have people sleeping all
over. It was enjoyable. . . . Holidays when navigation season
opened was just like any other day. Every day was the same.
Sundays, Saturdays, Tuesdays. Didn't make any difference.

There was one notable exception on the weekends.

Well, I should say that Saturdays and Sundays we didn't have
an eight o'clock meeting at the watch-standing room in the fog
signal building. . . . Monday through Friday we met at eight
o'clock in the morning at the watch-standing room. That was
about the only time that the three fellows would get together.
And we more or less planned the day. Some days we'd have a
fire drill. Other days we'd discuss, you know, when we were
going to do what. Such as cutting grass or painting or going
up and checking river lights or checking the main light at the
end of the canal or any general thing. These meetings didn't
last long. They did not exist on Saturday and Sunday.
Saturday and Sunday was, basically, you stood your watch
and that was it.

**For a short time the station managed with only two
men. This brought on extra responsibilities for the
families.**

When [civilian-in-charge] Mills retired, of course, there was

just Ben and myself and, of course, our families. And we had
to run the station, operate it, with two men at, really, the worst
time of the year, the spring of the year, when we were tending
the river or canal lights and range lights. Which meant that
those two men would have to check every light from the station
through to Princess Point, approximately three miles, and see
that the batteries were properly charged. We'd have to replace
them if [it] were necessary and paint them, maintain them.
And being a two-man job, naturally, left our station *un*manned.
Which [meant] our wives had to be so-called "trained" to turn
the horns on and turn the light on if necessary. But even at
worst we were only at the most a half an hour away from the
station at any one time.

*We had assigned days for doing
the wash so that there weren't
three people doing the wash on the
same day.*

Although they occasionally helped out when
necessary, family members had no official duties.

There was nothing expected of them by the government or by
the Coast Guard or the [civilian] keepers other than the normal,
expected cleanliness of houses. I mean, they weren't allowed
to have run-down things or anything like that. They had to
properly hang clothes even though we were an isolated station.
We had assigned days for doing the wash so that there weren't
three people doing the wash on the same day. . . . And at our

station it was set up so that it didn't interfere with anybody. It wasn't set up by order. All these things were planned out so that it fit into everybody's schedule.

At times, the work was harder than usual. One might think this would be during the harsh winters, but Don remembers otherwise.

Well, the most difficult time, I think, was in the beautiful weather of July and August. It may sound funny. But that, I think, would be the hardest time because there you were on the station and everybody is out there boating by, in their cruisers and enjoying themselves. And here you were, watch-standing.

Obtaining fresh vegetables was not a problem at the station. The families could barter with local farmers and therefore did not have their own gardens. But living at an isolated station required adjusting to different eating and shopping habits.

We didn't eat steaks or anything like that. When we had a steak, maybe once a month or once every couple months, that was great. You learn to live on hamburger. We didn't have freezers either. So, consequently, you couldn't go out and buy a large amount of meat and freeze it. You learn to live on staple items. We did have a lot of venison, a lot of fish. But as far as going out and buying roasts or that type of thing--you seemed to build your meals around potatoes and vegetables.

Lighthouse living required cooperation, resource-fulness and inventiveness. And the spirit of helping one's neighbor extended beyond the light station.

We helped the farmers, you know, if they needed a hand with something or we had something they needed from the station and we could help them with it, we helped them. . . . We helped one farmer build a barn. . . . There would be times we would run into something where we'd need a part or we'd need some ingenuity from somebody to put together something and keep it working. And we'd get in contact with the local people, farmers. Farmers in those days were used to temporary repairs made out of anything. Consequently, years ago, the Coast Guard was known as the "Bailing Wire Service" because they used anything and everything to keep your boat, keep your station operating. So, we used the ingenuity of the local people, the farmers. Which, that was their way of life, to help us, too. . . . It was interesting, too, to see if your--whatever you could dream up to make something work and then find out it actually did work. It was an accomplishment.

Keeping the light station in good condition--and the feeling of pride that accompanied it--was something the whole family enjoyed.

We kept the stations clean, spic and span. This was the way we were trained. This was the way we wanted it. We were proud of our stations. . . . We did take pride. And the families took pride. I don't say this was one hundred percent at all stations, but it was at the stations I was in contact with or was familiar with.

Max Gertz at home in Appleton, Wisconsin. (Photo courtesy of the Gertz family).

Maxwell Gertz

Max Gertz served in the U. S. Coast Guard for nearly twenty-four years. During the 1940s and 1950s he was stationed at several Lake Superior lighthouses including Sand Hills, Portage River (Jacobsville), Keweenaw Waterway Lower Entry, and Manitou Island, where he served for over nine years. Today, he and his wife, Serie, have homes in Lake Linden, Michigan, and Appleton, Wisconsin. He was interviewed on three separate occasions in February and March of 1986 by his daughter, Jean.

(Interviewer: Jean D. Gertz).

In 1935 Max applied to both the U. S. Lighthouse Service and the U. S. Coast Guard, which at the time were separate agencies. He heard from the Coast Guard first, entered the service, and went to his first life-saving station, Whitefish Point.

After reporting to Whitefish Point, after a month there, I got word from home that I was able to go into the Lighthouse Service. But it was a little too late then. I joined the Coast Guard. Finally, the Lighthouse [Service] was consolidated with the Coast Guard. So, I was happy at that time that my first choice would have been the Lighthouse.

After serving at other Coast Guard rescue stations, in 1940 he transferred to a light station for the first time.

Well, in 1939 [there was] the consolidation with the Lighthouse and the Coast Guard. There was an opening at Sand Hills light station. . . . When the radio beacons came in . . . that station was actually eliminated outside of the light. The foghorn and that was eliminated and the men were not needed there. . . . Your mother and I, we went up there and opened the station and stayed there, took care of the light that fall, and it was way in the latter part of November. Actually, we only used one section of the dwellings. Just a place that we needed. . . . There was no telephone out there. There was no communication of any sort.

After closing up the station, he returned to nearby Coast Guard stations, and for a short time served as a second assistant at Keweenaw WaterwayLower Entry light. In 1946 he transferred to Manitou Island light station, off the northern point of the Keweenaw Peninsula of Michigan. There were no family quarters at the island post, so the Gertz family stayed on the mainland.

Well, I was in charge. "Officer-in-charge," they called it. A little different than what they called the "lighthouse keeper," although that's what I was, the head lighthouse keeper. The different personnel with me were called "assistants." And when I first went there it was the twelfth of September and I had to learn everything about the station because sometime in the early part of December it meant that the station had to be closed. So, it meant that I had to do a lot of studying . . . and preparing the station for when the personnel and myself would leave there.

Other personnel would change during the nine seasons he spent at Manitou Island, but Max stayed on.

Well, it was kind of an unwritten law with the Service, out of Cleveland, Ninth Coast Guard District, that if you spent two navigational seasons at an isolated station you could almost ask for any place in the district. And if it was available they would transfer you there. They figured that two years on an isolated place like that would be enough for a person, although I stayed

---

They figured that two years on an isolated place like that would be enough for a person, although I stayed there nine and a half years. I liked it. I didn't request any change.

---

there nine and a half years. I liked it. I didn't request any change. . . . I would say the most anyone stayed there while I was there was three seasons. Two and a half seasons maybe. Always got transferred or asked for a transfer in the middle of the third season.

Although Manitou Island was considered an isolated station, Max did not feel isolated from his wife, family, and home on the mainland.

Well, I considered, myself, that I had more time at home--We had our own home in Hubbell. When I got stationed at Manitou Island, we purchased a home in Hubbell. Our family was there. So, I figured over the years that I was out at [Manitou]--and it was an isolated station with compensatory leave and I had my own annual leave that I was entitled to--that I considered myself, actually, home more than a person that would be working right, say, in the mines there or anything. And, we thought that [when] I got home we could do things that a person couldn't, actually, do with their family if they were, say, working nights and only had--or working days and nights, as a lot of them did at the mines there. I figured I had better time home with my family than people that worked around in the copper country.

The crew on Manitou Island was allowed to have visitors on occasion. Max sometimes let his daughters stay for a visit.

Oh, we had visitors out there, from time to time. Some of the personnel that were married that had their families or had a wife someplace--I know we had some as far as down in Tennessee--they would come up knowingly that they could come out and spend a week. But they were restricted to a certain time because it was, actually, a bachelor's station. No family quarters on there. . . . Well, a person could bring his . . . wife out. If they didn't live in the vicinity, that is, around the copper country, and visited, they could come out, and we had facilities there so that they could have their wife there for a short time. But regulations stated that it was only a bachelor's station, that you could only have your visitors there for a very short time. . . . [The station] was originally set up for a keeper--head keeper--and two assistants, plus there was another unit that was built onto the workshop for just visitors. The reason for that, I think--it was built there before I was there--in case of somebody with [a] small boat or something would get stranded and couldn't get back to the mainland for any reason or when they had technicians come out. That's another thing. We had technicians that came out. They had to have a place to stay. So that there was a unit there that was like a motel unit on the end of the workshop there, that the visitors could stay for a short time . It was mostly, I think, made for technicians that had to stay overnight or two or three days or whatever.

The men spent their free time at the station in various ways.

Well, some of the persons had hobbies there. I think, mostly, being that I'd be in the station a lot throughout the day, especially on a Sunday I'd prefer to get out and walk around on the island. It was too much of one day to walk completely around on the shoreline. There was no shoreline to speak of. It was all high rock, conglomerate rock. Very, very little beaches. But there was some beaches that were good that a person could do some agate picking. . . . We have a lot of nice agates that was made into jewelry that was gotten off of Manitou, off the beaches there.

. . . Well, even some of [the crew would] be playing solitaire if nothing else--but some of them went to model building. And that's not the kind of models they have now. They would start right from scratch with balsa wood. . . . They would do their own modeling. Boats and airplanes. Mostly airplanes. We also had recreation there, like baseball gloves and that. They'd play catch and that. There was no way that you could do any batting of any sort because, besides the woods and the rocks, the lake was very close. It wouldn't be long and you'd be right out there. But they'd play catch.

Although far from grocery stores and the conveniences of a town, the crew at Manitou did not lack for good food.

Oh, the fishing was great. Some of the best. I have to tell you this: when you'd go out there in, oh, like I said, the latter part of March, first part of April, there was a cookstove that was started then. (And it was oil, like you'd have like in a restaurant, you might say. Just steel plate.) And that [stove] was started there [in March] and went day and night till we left there sometime in December. And the reason for it, we could use it for heat. It heated the building. Plus, the bean crock

Plus, the bean crock was always going and we had the best of lake trout.

was always going and we had the best of lake trout. The real, natural lake trout. You could take a skiff out front and row around for five minutes, come in with a three to five pound nice lake trout, prepare it, put it on a cookie sheet, and put it in an oven and broil it in there, and it was the best.

.

The daily routine of work at the station included the maintenance of various kinds of equipment and a lot of paperwork for the officer-in-charge.

That's one thing that I never liked about the whole thing was the paperwork. Naturally, a lot of people don't care too much about paperwork. . . . We had two big air compressors in the engine room that was for the foghorn. . . . And then there was three generators and a big bank of batteries. Everything run off of a hundred and ten [electric current] . . . and a generator had to be going day and night. So, all those machinery had to be serviced, and oil had to be changed constantly. And we had a large supply of spare parts in case of trouble. Plus, if anybody knows living around the water, that painting and deterioration of the buildings around the water is more so than inland. Plus, the light had to be maintained. . . . Well, that all had to be polished and kept right up to--oh, boy. Oh, every day there was a man up there [who] had to check it out to make sure that that light operated properly . . . and the lens were clean, and all the brass. You had a lot of work on the inside. The tower, it seemed like it was forever that it needed attention inside because of the condensation. See, that was a skeleton tower, at Manitou, connected with the dwelling. So, the heat from the dwelling would go up through the tower and we couldn't keep the windows in the tower open all the time, so, there was condensation forming in there, and it was a constant job to keep the inside of that tower properly maintained.

To make the task of daily paperwork more efficient, Max created his own record keeping system.

I started a form there. It was called the "Abstract of
Operations." I started my own form. The Service had one that
you had to submit once a year. And that was a summary of
everything that was used at the station. . . . I formed another
one that was a form that I used every day. It was kept up every
day, that you didn't have to go through all the records at the
end of the year to make up this "Abstract of Operations." I
kept it up from day to day. So, at the end of the year, that had
to be sent in. That was for the Service to indicate, throughout
the whole Service, how much money they'd have to budget to
keep all the stations operating. So, that had to go in right after
the fiscal year. . . . The district would know exactly how much
that station would require and the supplies that was needed.
That would be fuel, that'd be paintbrushes, paint, soap that
was needed, toilet paper. You could name it. Everything that
you'd use at a home. Plus, all the engines, all the necessary
lubricating oils, all the gasoline that was used for the boat.
Well, you could name anything and it had to be--We'd have a
record of that. And to go through the whole record of what we
used throughout the year, this form I got together, I think,
helped a lot, so that I had it right up to date, from day to day.

**In addition to keeping records of supplies, he was
responsible for keeping a daily journal.**

Oh, you had to write a daily log. I wrote the daily log. And
when I wasn't there, the next in charge, the assistant, would
write the log. . . . Once a day, at the end of the [day]--And I
always took the watch from eight to midnight, evening, and
from eight in the morning till noon. And those two watches I
always took. And that gave me a chance during the watch,
from eight to midnight watch, to bring that log up to date for
the end of that day. And everything that happened that was any
value at all for the station--any maintenance of the equipment--

was all written in the log at that time. Plus, the weather.

When the crew prepared Manitou Island lighthouse for the winter they had to shut down their cookstove and delicious bean pot.

There was quite a bit to do for preparing the station for winter closing. Even, like I said before, we finally had to turn off the kitchen range. Boy, that kitchen range really did a duty from day to night from the time we got there till the time we left. Well, it kept the building nice and warm and was always set to do some cooking. Fact is, the bean crock was going all the time. We had a great big bean crock and when that would get down to the last cupful, why, that was taken out and washed and a new set was put together. . . . I know a lot of fellows that would come in off of watch--well, myself even--at midnight. Boy, you'd be hungry. So, I'd dish out a bowlful of nice baked beans. Oh, boy, those beans were good, I'm telling you! You talk about Boston baked beans. They [the lighthouse crew] had it just as good or better.

*Jim Goudreau giving a tour on October 25, 1985 at the top of
the Seul Choix lighthouse near Gulliver, Michigan, where he
currently resides as caretaker. (Photo by Tom Kozma).*

James A. Goudreau

*After growing up at several Lake Michigan lighthouses
and a long career in the Navy, Jim Goudreau is now a
lighthouse keeper himself. Since 1975 he has been
the live-in caretaker of the Seul Choix lighthouse
grounds, now a park for Mueller township, near
Gulliver, Michigan. His father, William Goudreau, was a
lighthouse keeper from circa 1935 until his death in
1967. He retired from the Seul Choix lighthouse. Jim
spent his childhood during the 1930s and 1940s at
South Fox Island and Poverty Island lighthouses. His
father also served at the Green Bay Crib light. Jim was
interviewed at the Seul Choix lighthouse on October
25, 1985.*

(Interviewer: LuAnne Gaykowski Kozma).

Jim remembers when his father quit the fishing industry
of the Seul Choix Point area and chose the life of a
lighthouse keeper.

My father had been a commercial fisherman. And when Port
Inland Lime and Stone Company opened up in '33 he worked
there. And then he applied for the Lighthouse [Service] and it
was either '34 or '35 he went into the Lighthouse [Service].
And we started. The first place we went to was South Fox
Island. And we left here at [Seul Choix] Point in a fish boat,
took all our earthly possessions, and off we went. . . . On Fox

Island we were in a three-family house. Dad was the third assistant, so, we lived upstairs in one end of it.

The station on South Fox Island at that time required four lighthouse employees. The Goudreau family had to adjust to life on an island as well as to the schedules of lighthouse work. The family was especially careful to prepare and store enough food.

On Fox Island we came on shore only on the fifteenth of the month. The keeper and the second assistant came in on the first of the month, for seven days. The first assistant and the third assistant came in on the fifteenth. That's the way they split it up. And you bought food for a month.

The first place we went to was South Fox Island. And we left here at the Point in a fish boat, took all our earthly possessions, and off we went.

. . . Now, you sent a list in on the first for those people. And they brought, like, your meat and stuff out. We ate a lot of homemade, canned foods. Dad would buy a half a cow and Ma would can it. Or she'd can wild rabbit or partridge, or can fish. She canned a pig one time. I remember that very clear. It hung in the basement.

Jim Goudreau's family arrived on South Fox Island in circa 1935 with "all their earthly possessions" in a fishing boat, and with the help of some neighbors from the mainland. Above, young Jim (standing on rock), his mother, and the neighbors pose for a picture on the day they arrived on South Fox Island. The skeletal lighthouse tower is in the background. (Photo taken by Jim's father. Courtesy of Jim Goudreau).

Living at a Lighthouse

... We were on Poverty [Island] that year and Dad went
ashore and bought a pig and brought it out, hung it in the
basement. Now, he had it dressed, but he didn't have it cut
up. . . . So, Ma wanted it canned, so she just went down and
cut chunks of it off and canned it as time went on.

We had a garden on Fox Island. The garden was about five
miles away from the lighthouse. You had to walk down the
beach and then back into the woods.

Jim and his mother spent summers on the islands and
the winter months with family back on the mainland at
Seul Choix Point. At South Fox Island, he was the only
child; at Poverty Island, he was one of many children.
Jim enjoyed having the best of both worlds.

I liked it at the lighthouse because I had the freedom, but I liked
it in town because there were kids. . . . After being here [on the
mainland] all winter it was fun to go out there. By July, I was
hoping to come back. On Poverty, I didn't care if I ever left
there because there were all kinds of kids and we did all kinds
of things. It was unusual to be out on a lighthouse with only
one [kid]. That was unusual. At Poverty, Floyd Miller had
eight or nine [kids], and Johnson had six, I think. . . .That was
a haven, man, to come from Fox Island, with no kids, to
Poverty Island, with all the kids in the world.

Allowing children in the tower and near the expensive
lens and lighting equipment was not permitted.
Although Jim was taught how to light the lamps, he was
not expected to assist with lighting, or to polish the lens.

Oh, yeah, I could light it. You betcha. They wouldn't let me touch it. Oh, my god, that would be sacrilegious to go up there and touch the lights. No, I might put fingerprints on the lens or something. Can't do that.

No, no. That was one of the things they told me, you know, "Don't touch the lens. You'll ruin them, the prisms in there. Oh, you'll leave fingerprints on it. We'll never get them out." And all that sort of thing. I never touched them. "Don't touch the brass 'cause it eats holes right in the brass." It was just to keep me away from it, more than anything else. Beautiful solid brass fittings that they keep all these prisms in. You know, that was fascinating. It looked like gold it was so pretty. And they wanted to keep me away from it. So, I did.

And they wouldn't let you in the towers to start with, unless you went up with your dad or one of the other guys. Occasionally you'd sneak in.

For the children at Poverty Island lighthouse, keeping out of trouble was difficult. The island was small, and there were many rules to follow.

. . . The kids were a major problem. They had a couple tha⁺ were like the Katzenjammer kids; they were in constant trouble. And on [Poverty] Island they had an old--it was a big steel tank that they had cut a door in, and used it for a coal bin. And that was the "prison" for the kids. When you did something wrong, they put you in the "coal bin" and closed the door and locked it. You may stay there an hour, you may stay there all afternoon. It depends on what you did. . . . Well, there was very little coal left in it 'cause they had other places to store it. But it was just an old coal bin. Yeah, there was coal in it, so you got pretty black occasionally. But when they closed the

door it was dark in there also. So that, you could hear
somebody [say], "You're going to the coal bin," you knew
somebody had messed up, real bad, that they were going to the
coal bin. . . . [Kids would] steal tools. You know, the men 'd
be working and kids would run by and grab a wrench and off
they'd go, to fix something of their own, you know. And the
guys are working with it. Get in the paint shop, you know,
break out a bucket of paint, start painting something that wasn't
supposed to be painted. All kinds of--little stuff that,
really--the kids don't really think that they're in trouble for it,
but, the men don't like it. Find a bucket of old paint that got
throwed out. "Oh, there's a little bit of paint left in it." And
you're painting on the sidewalk, you know? Drawing pictures.
Well, you didn't paint the sidewalks. This kind of stuff. . . .
Yeah, I spent some hours in the coal bin! I think everybody
did. Girls and all. There was nobody exempt from it. You
got in trouble, you went in the coal bin.

Work at a lighthouse was not always a solitary
experience. Teamwork was required when doing
many lighthouse chores at a large station. As Jim
explains:

You might dislike somebody very much, but you still had to
work with them. Now that happened pretty regular because
you're together all the time. The men worked together
constantly. You couldn't do a job just by yourself. So, you
had to work together. . . . For example, in painting this tower.
The scaffolding that went around it, it took all three men to do
it. . . . So, you better work together fairly decent.

As at other stations, the wives sometimes helped with

the work.

A lot of the women used to stand watches for the men. They'd [the men] work all day, and then you still had your watches to stand. . . . If they happened to be working extra hard or something, needed a little extra rest, like unloading a supply ship or something like this. Maybe they had a mid-watch. So, the wife might get up and--All you were doing was watching the weather, make sure the light was on. And if the fog started moving in, you'd call the husband and he'd go turn the fog signal on.

The men worked together constantly. You couldn't do a job just by yourself. So, you had to work together.

One could do a variety of things to keep busy while on watch.

We had one guy when we were out there [South Fox Island], he used to knit his own socks. He didn't want anybody to know, but they found out. He would tear a sock apart and reknit it. He was a single man. His socks looked like they were store-bought. They were beautiful socks.

Besides the relatively easy work of standing watches, a

keeper and assistants had a lot of hard labor to do. Jim
was a full grown youngster and eager to help the men
on South Fox Island.

As a kid, I would help a little bit, you know, as much as they'd
let me. Mow some grass or trim a little bit. Carry stuff for
them. I was the only kid out there. . . . I remember working
with the working parties that brought the stuff ashore. Because
everything was brought in on barges. They'd bring it in to the
dock. Like your kerosene or your gasolines were all brought
in fifty-five-gallon drums. And they'd roll them rascals all up
them hills and dump them in the big storage tanks, which was
an awful job for these guys, young sailors off the lighthouse
tenders. So, I'd pitch right in and help them.

The lighthouse tenders also brought the team of
inspectors. Jim recalls the team would stay for a day or
two and survey the entire station. Not a single detail
was overlooked.

Oh, they'd check all the grounds, all the property. Well, like
they'd check your fence line if you had a fence. They had big
fences across here. They'd walk the fences and to make sure
that the concrete blocks at the end that had "U. S. Lighthouse
Establishment" on it were still in place. All kinds of stuff.
Make sure all the windows were puttied. Very, very particular.
. . . Maybe four or five guys would come. Each one would
have his own area to check. They'd also check all the books,
because you had a lot of paperwork you had to do.

The keepers paid attention to those small details and
sometimes took extra steps to impress the inspectors.

Living at a Lighthouse

Usually they had a tool board set up with all the tools on it.
You never used 'em. They had another box of tools they used.
That was for *show*. But they were there. Every tool that you
would use would be there.

At the South Fox Island station there was extra work to
do because there were two lighthouse towers, the older
one considered as a back-up.

They maintained the old one like they did the new one.
Because they never removed it. It was still there. If it was
there you maintained it! They just never turned it on. But they
kept the lens clean and the windows washed and the shades up.
It was ready to go. Instantly.

The keepers' families on South Fox Island spent only a
moderate amount of time socializing.

The women talked most of the time. The guys would talk as
they were working together. And then, maybe, they might
come over for an evening and play some cards. Not too often.
You were too *close*. You were right together all the time.

Only occasionally would lighthouse keepers at different
stations in the area see each other. The Goudreau
family took trips mostly to visit relatives and an old
lighthouse buddy of Jim's father.

Oh, yeah, most of the lighthouse guys knew all the other ones.
Yeah, they knew who they were. They would meet 'em

periodically. When we were on Fox Island the closest one was
South Manitou. You know, that's a long ways away. And
you didn't have time to go down there and jaw for an hour or
so. You're talking two or three hours in the boat. So, you
didn't go any place.

Now, when we [went] downstate, we used to stop at Big Point
Sable [lighthouse] and visit with a guy that used to be on Fox
Island, Mr. Timmer. We'd stop in there periodically. . . .
After I was in the service, Dad used to take a month off and
he'd come out and visit me in California or wherever I was.
And first place he'd go is down to the docks or to the
lighthouse. You know, he was an ex-fisherman and he was a
"Lighthouse," so he'd go visit those people. And he liked that.

Afterword

These interview excerpts are just some of the many memorable stories former residents tell about everyday life at the Great Lakes lighthouses. The Great Lakes Lighthouse Keepers Association (GLLKA) encourages lighthouse sites, museums, and historical agencies to document the lives of former employees and residents of lighthouses through oral history interviews. GLLKA's 31-page "Oral History Interviewing Manual" is available for $5.00 to interested groups and individuals. GLLKA would appreciate information from others who have conducted similar programs at lighthouse sites. Anyone who would like to participate in GLLKA's ongoing oral history program, "Living at a Lighthouse: Oral Histories from the Great Lakes," or who would like to donate tapes of previously conducted interviews to the tape collection, please contact:

Great Lakes Lighthouse Keepers Association
P.O. Box 80
Allen Park, MI 48101

Index